Equality Bill

Equality Impact Assessment

December 2009

ISBN: 9780108508714

Printed in the UK by The Stationery Office Limited
on behalf of the Controller of Her Majesty's Stationery Office

ID P002337878   12/09   928   19585

Printed on paper containing 75% recycled fibre content minimum.

Equality Bill
Equality Impact Assessment

Introduction

This Equality Impact Assessment considers the impact of the measures in the Equality Bill as re-presented in the fifth session of Parliament, in terms of their impact on race, age, disability, sex, gender reassignment, sexual orientation and religion or belief.

The aim is to ensure that the implications for equality for all the protected characteristics[1] have been properly assessed during the development of the policy, taking account of views expressed, and to provide assurance that changes needed to mitigate any potential adverse impacts have been identified. Although the current legal requirements[2] to assess impacts on equality relate only to race, disability and gender[3], this document also considers the impacts on age, religion or belief, gender reassignment and sexual orientation, in line with the integrating policy of the Bill.

The Equality Impact Assessment follows the Equality and Human Rights Commission guidance. It has been updated from the Equality Impact Assessment published in April 2009 on introduction of the Equality Bill.

Context and drivers for the Equality Bill

The Government established the Discrimination Law Review in February 2005 to consider the opportunities for creating a clearer and more streamlined legislative framework, which produces better

---

[1] Note: For the purposes of the Equality Impact Assessment, the protected characteristic of gender incorporates pregnancy and maternity, and marriage and civil partnership unless otherwise stated.
[2] Under the Race Relations Act 1976 (as amended), the Disability Discrimination Act 1995 (as amended) and the Sex Discrimination Act 1975 (as amended).
[3] The gender equality duty applies in part to gender reassignment.

outcomes for those who experience disadvantage.

A separate independent Equalities Review, led by Trevor Phillips, looked at the broader issues leading to an unequal society, in particular the reasons why inequalities persist in certain areas and for certain groups of people and communities, despite some forty years of equality legislation. It issued an interim report in March 2006 and its final report to the Prime Minister in February 2007[4]. The Equalities Review recognised that legislation against discrimination is a significant lever in producing changes in social and cultural attitudes and behaviour affecting equality.

In July 2008 the Government published a comprehensive Government Response to its 2007 Equality Bill consultation[5], which summarised the responses received and set out revised policy proposals.

The basic rationale behind the Equality Bill is to streamline and strengthen discrimination law in Great Britain. Its main objectives are to:

Strengthen the law by:

- Banning age discrimination in the provision of goods, facilities and services and in the exercise of public functions. This is not about stopping older people enjoying free bus passes, it is about tackling age discrimination where it has negative consequences. A further specific consultation about possible exceptions in this area was carried out from June to

---

[4] http://archive.cabinetoffice.gov.uk/equalitiesreview/
[5] http://www.equalities.gov.uk/PDF/EqBillGovResponse.pdf

September 2009 and there will be a further consultation on draft regulations and a transition period before the prohibition is implemented.

- Protecting people if they experience discrimination because of a combination of two relevant protected characteristics, for example as a black woman, which they would not experience as being either black, or a woman. This is called dual discrimination.

- Increasing transparency, for example by banning secrecy clauses which prevent people discussing their own pay; and by providing a power to require gender pay gap reporting by some employers[6]. Greater transparency will help to tackle persistent inequalities like the gender pay gap which stands at 22.6%.

- Extending the scope for positive action. This is a chance for employers to make their workforce more diverse when choosing between two job candidates of equal merit. All other things being equal, a head teacher in a mixed-sex school, for example, may decide to appoint a man if there were no male teachers in the school. This could benefit boys who would gain a role model they can relate to.

- Extending the period during which women-only shortlists are allowed. This will help to increase the representation of women in Parliament and elected bodies.

---

[6] The intention is that this power would be used if insufficient progress is made by 2013. The power would apply to employers with 250 or more employees.

- Strengthening enforcement, for example, by allowing tribunals to make wider recommendations in discrimination cases. This will help to tackle institutional discrimination by enabling the whole workforce to benefit from improvements after an individual wins a discrimination claim.

- Requiring some public bodies to consider socio-economic inequalities when making strategic decisions about priorities.

Streamline the law by:

- Distilling nine pieces of legislation into a single Act. A clearer legal framework for equality will be easier to understand and implement, particularly for businesses at a time when resources are stretched.

- Creating a single new Equality Duty[7] on public bodies to have due regard to the need to eliminate unlawful discrimination, advance equality of opportunity and foster good community relations. The new duty will cover race, disability and gender, as now, but also include age, sexual orientation, religion or belief, pregnancy and maternity explicitly and fully cover gender reassignment; thus replacing the three existing, separate duties with a single, more effective framework. The Government carried out a further consultation from June to end September 2009 on which specific duties should underpin the general duty.

---

[7] The public sector Equality Duty will not be an absolute duty to take action but will require public authorities to consider and address equality issues in all their functions, insofar as is relevant and proportionate.

- Simplifying the definition of disability discrimination so people are clear whether they are protected.

Support wider work to promote equality which includes:

- Ensuring the public sector has due regard to equality when buying goods and services. Every year around £220 billion is spent by the public sector on goods and services supplied by the private sector. This purchasing power can be put to good use to improve equality. The Bill contains a power to impose specific duties on certain public authorities[8] to include equality in their considerations when carrying out procurement activities.

The Government is committed to there being no regression of rights overall, so that the protection currently afforded by the law will generally be maintained, with some changes to increase its effectiveness. In addition to retaining existing levels of protection, the Equality Bill will extend protection to new areas where this is necessary and justified, therefore benefiting those who currently have lower levels of protection.

The Bill will extend primarily to Great Britain.

The existing legislative framework concerning discrimination

The current domestic legislative framework concerning discrimination comprises a number of separate pieces of

---

[8] These are public authorities that are "contracting authorities" within the meaning of the EU Public Sector Directive: Directive 2004/18/EC of the European Parliament and of the Council of 31 March 2004 on the coordination of procedures for the award of public works contract, public supply contracts and public service contracts.

legislation enacted over the past forty years. The first were the Race Relations Acts of 1965 and 1968. These were followed in 1970 by the Equal Pay Act. The main subsequent statutes (amended as appropriate) are:

- the Sex Discrimination Act 1975;

- the Race Relations Act 1976;

- the Disability Discrimination Act 1995;

- the Employment Equality (Religion or Belief) Regulations 2003;

- the Employment Equality (Sexual Orientation) Regulations 2003;

- the Equality Act 2006 which set up the Equality and Human Rights Commission and extended protection against discrimination outside the workplace on grounds of religion or belief;

- the Employment Equality (Age) Regulations 2006; and

- the Equality Act (Sexual Orientation) Regulations 2007.

Methodology

This Equality Impact Assessment is unusual in the sense that the entire purpose of its subject – the Equality Bill – is to tackle discrimination and promote equality of opportunity. It therefore looks at the impact of particular Bill measures, both in terms of their effect, if any, across equality strands[9] and in terms of their effect on particular strands where such an impact has been identified. The questions considered are primarily whether a proposal affects the equality strands equally or differently and whether the strands are affected in a positive or negative way.

The Equality Bill was developed by the Government Equalities Office in consultation with a wide range of government departments and stakeholders including equality representatives, trades unions and business. [10]

The preliminary proposals for the Equality Bill were consulted on in a consultation paper entitled 'A Framework for Fairness: Proposals for a single Equality Bill for Great Britain' between June 2007 and September 2007[11]. During the consultation period we held five general public consultation events around Great Britain as well as an event focusing on public sector equality duties and an event specifically aimed at business. In addition, bilateral meetings were held with key stakeholders, including the previous Equality

---

[9] Race, age, disability, sex, gender reassignment, sexual orientation, religion or belief.
[10] The 2007 consultation received responses from around 600 organisations (on the Government Equalities Office website at
http://www.equalities.gov.uk/default.aspx?page=1120) and 4000 individuals.
[11] http://www.equalities.gov.uk/default.aspx?page=1162 Further formal consultations have been carried out since them, on age discrimination and specific equality duties, as well as engagement with stakeholders on specific issues such as dual discrimination.

Commissions (the Commission for Racial Equality, the Disability Rights Commission, the Equal Opportunities Commission) and subsequently the Equality and Human Rights Commission and equality representatives including Age Concern, Help the Aged, the Equality and Diversity Forum and others.

We received over 4,000 responses to the consultation, including 600 from organisations. Following the consultation the Government Equalities Office, DWP officials and Ministers have engaged extensively with various stakeholders representing a wide range of equality interests.

The Government Equalities Office has also established a Senior Stakeholder Group whose main function has been to discuss the Bill as it has developed. The Group meets monthly and its membership consists of key equality and business stakeholders[12].

In addition, research was commissioned in the form of a comparative study of legal systems addressing equality and discrimination in different countries, including South Africa and Canada. The Government Equalities Office also co-sponsored research by Schneider-Ross into the impact of the existing public sector equality duties and subsequently commissioned further research in this area.

In 2008 the Department of Health published the findings of two literature reviews and two research studies on the nature and extent of age discrimination in the provision of health and social care and the costs and benefits of eliminating it. The purpose of

---

[12] Full membership of the Senior Stakeholder Group can be found at
http://www.equalities.gov.uk/equality_bill/senior_stakeholder_group.aspx

the research was to inform decisions on whether or not to legislate on age discrimination outside the workplace. In addition, a Financial Services Working Group reported in autumn 2008 on the possible impact of the prohibition on age discrimination on financial services; and the Department of Health established in late 2008 an advisory group of stakeholders to support work on preparing health and social care services to adapt to the prohibition on age discrimination.   In April 2009, the then Secretary of State for Health asked Sir Ian Carruthers (Chief Executive of the South West Strategic Health Authority) and Jan Ormondroyd (Chief Executive of Bristol City Council) jointly to lead a national review of age discrimination in health and social care. The review was based in the South West region but addressed the implementation of the ban on age discrimination and the public sector equality duty across England. Following the review the Secretary of State for Health, said that he supports the recommendations and that the age discrimination ban in the Equality Bill should apply for health and social care in 2012.

Structure of this document

This document broadly follows the structure of the Equality Bill itself.

Chapter 1:

Duty on some public authorities to consider socio-economic inequality

1.1   The Equality Bill provides a power to introduce a range of measures (specific duties) to ensure that public authorities address discrimination arising from the protected characteristics, namely race, gender, or disability. But inequality might not just come from a person's gender or ethnicity, sexual orientation or disability. Co-existing and interwoven with such specific inequalities lies the persistent inequality which arises from socio-economic disadvantage. While there are Public Service Agreement[13] targets and indicators across Government to narrow gaps arising from social class and income, there is currently no over-arching requirement on public authorities to address the inequality associated with these factors - where people live, their family background or the job they do.

1.2   Research has shown that a person's socio-economic circumstances at birth are unfortunately still a very strong predictor of his/her future success in life.

1.3   The Equality Bill therefore introduces a new duty on key public authorities to tackle the unequal outcomes that are associated with socio-economic disadvantage. The duty applies only to the broad, strategic decisions that organisations take, and not to their decisions about individuals, or in regard to very specific service-delivery issues. It is intended to be unbureaucratic, giving some flexibility to public bodies themselves to decide best how to meet it. There are no statutory, process-related requirements – in terms of prescribed schemes or reports – to underpin it. However, the Government will publish guidance setting out what issues we would expect public bodies to consider in regard to the duty.

Stakeholder engagement

1.4 Our discussions with stakeholders, and a great deal of research, have shown the extent to which socio-economic disadvantage is closely related, in many cases, to individual equality strands. For example:

- around 80% of people from black and minority ethnic (BME) backgrounds live in the 88 most deprived local authority wards in the country[14];

- disabled adults are twice as likely to live in low-income households as non-disabled adults[15];

- half of all lone parents are on a low income, the overwhelming majority of them being women[16];

- only 65% of Indian Muslim men have jobs, compared to 78% of White British Christian men, and 74% of Indian Hindu men[17].

---

[13] Public Service Agreement: department targets to achieve priority objectives.
[14] Office of National Statistics (2003): 2001 Census, [National Report].
[15] Households Below Average Income 1994/95 – 2006/07, Department for Work and Pensions

<u>General impacts</u>

1.5   As the statistics above show, there is clear evidence that, to a greater or lesser extent, socio-economic disadvantage disproportionately affects people from ethnic minorities, older people, disabled people, women, and people of certain religions. The new duty to tackle socio-economic inequality will have a positive impact on these groups by ensuring consideration is given to measures to address the disadvantage they face and reinforcing work that is already being done to tackle inequalities for some of these groups, for example under the public sector equality duties.

1.6   The new duty should also have positive impacts on groups which would not generally be the focus of action under the equality duties. For example, among children eligible for free school meals, white children performed worse than almost any other ethnic group at GCSE, with only 17% getting 5 or more good GCSE passes (including English and Maths), compared to 59% of eligible Chinese pupils, and 42% of eligible Indian pupils. Children from socio-economically disadvantaged backgrounds are one obvious group that this new legislation will benefit.

1.7   The new duty will therefore enhance and support the existing equality duties and the new single Public Sector Equality Duty being introduced in the Bill. It will ensure that public bodies should consider socio-economic

---

[16] Households Below Average Income 1994/95 – 2006/07, Department for Work and Pensions

[17] Census 2001, Office for National Statistics

inequalities regardless of who is affected by them. This will both help those experiencing disadvantage – who in many cases will have characteristics protected by the Public Sector Equality Duty – and help to counter the perception that some groups currently get preferential treatment solely on the basis of those characteristics.

Chapter 2:

Simplifying and harmonising definitions and tests in discrimination law

2.1   The Equality Bill simplifies and harmonises existing definitions and concepts used in the different pieces of discrimination law covering different protected groups wherever possible. The Bill's simplification measures are based on the following principles:

- existing levels of protection should be retained overall;

- common approaches should be adopted wherever practicable;

- the law should be practical and reflect the realities of people's everyday lives and the way business operates; and

- British discrimination law should meet the requirements of European law.

Definition of sex discrimination

2.2   The Equality Bill makes clear that it is direct sex discrimination, outside the workplace, to treat a breastfeeding mother unfavourably even beyond the period of six months when protection against maternity discrimination outside the workplace applies.

Impact on gender

2.3　　This will have positive equality implications for women because it will remove any doubt that mothers are protected when, for example, accessing goods and services, from being discriminated against because they are breastfeeding. Currently, mothers of young children may be deterred from breastfeeding because they fear being turned out of public places if they seek to breastfeed a child.

2.4　　The Equality Bill gives mothers certainty that they would be protected if they were turned away from a café, for example, or told to get off a bus just because they were breastfeeding.

Definition of gender reassignment

2.5　　The Equality Bill removes from the definition of gender reassignment the current reference to 'medical supervision' to make it clear that protection against discrimination is not dependent upon a person being under medical supervision.

Impact on gender reassignment

2.6　　The clear message from the consultation was that many people believe that the requirement of being under 'medical supervision' in the current definition of gender reassignment means that protection is only provided after reassignment surgery. This has meant that people with gender dysphoria who have been living their lives in their acquired gender, perhaps for a long time, but have never sought any medical advice, considered themselves to be excluded from protection from discrimination.

2.7   By removing the requirement of being under 'medical supervision' from the definition, the Equality Bill makes clear that protection from gender reassignment discrimination covers those people who are committed to living their lives in the gender opposite to their birth gender, with or without surgical intervention. This will have a positive impact on equality for transsexual people.

Direct discrimination and harassment - association and perception

2.8   The Equality Bill extends protection against direct discrimination and harassment based on association and perception to the protected characteristics and certain areas where this does not currently apply or only partly applies – namely, to disability, sex, gender reassignment and age.

2.9   These extensions accord with the harmonisation objectives of the Bill and also implement requirements of the 2008 "Coleman judgment" by the European Court of Justice[18].

Impact on disability

2.10   Extending protection from direct discrimination and harassment to people who are discriminated against or harassed because they are wrongly perceived to be disabled or because of their association with a disabled person will have a positive impact on disabled people and their families and carers, and on people who might be treated badly because they are wrongly thought to be disabled.

Impact on age

2.11   Discrimination based on someone's perceived age is already unlawful in employment. The Equality Bill extends this prohibition to other areas, for example, the provision of goods, facilities and services and the exercise of public functions and will also outlaw discrimination against someone because of their association with a person of a particular age both in the workplace and beyond. (This applies to people aged 18 and over).

2.12   In relation to discrimination because of association, an employer would not, for example, be able to treat an employee less favourably (this might be by refusing to promote that employee) because the employee had an elderly or younger relative needing care (unless the employer could objectively justify this treatment). As with disability, the impact is likely to be greatest for those with caring responsibilities.

2.13   The extension of protection against discrimination in relation to perception, in practice, means that it would be unlawful to exclude an otherwise fit person from certain

---

[18] See Annex A for details.

facilities or services simply because they "look too old".
(This only applies to those aged 18 and over).

Impact on race

2.14   Protection against discrimination and harassment already
        extends not only to members of a particular racial group,
        but also to people who may be wrongly perceived to be
        members of that racial group; and to people who are
        associated with members of a particular racial group.

Impact on gender

2.15   Individuals will in future be able to seek redress if they are
        directly discriminated against or harassed because they:

        ▪ associate with someone of a particular sex; or

        ▪ are wrongly perceived as being of a particular sex.

2.16   For example, a man who is denied promotion because his
        reference is written by a woman line manager who is
        assumed to be less credible than male managers would
        be able to claim discrimination because of association
        with a woman. A young man who applies for a job, but is
        not considered because the employer mistakes his name
        for that of a woman and the employer does not want
        young women working for him in case they become
        pregnant, would be protected.

Impact on gender reassignment

2.17   Individuals will be able to seek redress if they are directly discriminated against or harassed because they:

- associate with someone who is planning to undergo, is undergoing or has undergone gender reassignment; or

- are wrongly perceived as planning to undergo, undergoing or having undergone gender reassignment.

2.18 Providing protection against discrimination based on association is assumed to have a positive impact on equality for people who associate with transsexual people.

2.19 In its Response to the Equality Bill consultation the Government indicated that it did not propose to extend protection to include people wrongly perceived to be transsexual. However, many respondents, including transgendered individuals and groups representing their interests, felt that this protection should be provided. It was felt that a person could be wrongly perceived to be transsexual if their physical and/or vocal characteristics did not conform to the societal perception of what is 'the norm' for their sex. Such discrimination could also occur in the provision of goods and services, where providers may be more likely to discriminate on the basis of perceived gender reassignment.

2.20 In the light of the further representations made by trans organisations, and in view of the need to extend protection in any event as a result of the Coleman judgment[19] , the Equality Bill extends protection on the basis of perceived gender reassignment. This provides new protection for individuals who have gender dysphoria, but who have not yet made the permanent transition to live in the opposite gender and are considered as being transvestite. It will also cover some people with intersex conditions (physical, chromosonal, genetic and hormonal conditions which may cause intermediate or atypical combinations of physical features that usually distinguish male from female) and others who may have an ambiguous gender appearance.

Indirect discrimination

2.21   The Equality Bill removes inconsistencies in the definition of indirect discrimination used in existing discrimination legislation, for example in respect of gender and race.

Impact on gender

2.22   On indirect discrimination on grounds of sex, there is a notable inconsistency within the Sex Discrimination Act 1975 where two different definitions apply depending on whether or not provisions are governed by EU Directives. The Equality Bill removes this inconsistency, making it easier for people to know their rights and responsibilities in this area.

Impact on gender reassignment

2.23   The Bill extends protection against indirect discrimination

---

[19] For details see Annex A

so that it covers gender reassignment both inside and outside the workplace, which will make for greater legal consistency and an increase in protection for transsexual people.

Victimisation

2.24 The Equality Bill removes the current requirement for a comparator in victimisation cases (i.e. a person in comparison with whom the victim has been treated badly). Instead, the victim will only need to show he/she has suffered harm. It also harmonises protection against victimisation for children in schools where their parent or sibling makes a complaint, for example, about discrimination or harassment. Currently such protection from "proxy victimisation"[20] only exists where such a complaint relates to disability. This will be extended to cover all grounds.

General impact

2.25 Positioning discrimination law on the same basis as employment law, which does not in every case require a comparator to be identified in order to prove victimisation, should remove a barrier to some claims. It will still be necessary to show that victimisation occurred directly as a result of the claimant doing or being suspected of doing a protected act. These changes should have a positive impact on equality for all protected characteristics.

---

[20] This is where a person does a protected act (such as a complaint about discrimination or harassment) under the legislation, but someone else is victimised as a result.

2.26   Extending protection from "proxy victimisation" for children in schools will have a positive impact on equality for all the protected grounds except disability, where this protection already exists.

Removing inconsistencies in race discrimination legislation

2.27   There are a number of inconsistencies within the Race Relations Act 1976 (as amended) resulting from the way in which the 2000 Race Directive was transposed into domestic law. This has led to a two-tier form of protection with, for example, the newer formulation of indirect discrimination, the new statutory definition of harassment and the reversed burden of proof applying to race and ethnic or national origins, but not to colour or nationality.

<u>Impact on race</u>

2.28   The Equality Bill extends the provisions which apply to race or national origins so that they also cover colour and nationality, so that protection is offered on the same terms for all forms of racial discrimination. This will have a positive impact because the grounds on which people are protected will be much clearer and the protection will be more extensive.

Chapter 3:

Protecting against age discrimination outside the workplace

3.1   The Employment Equality (Age) Regulations 2006 provide protection against discrimination on grounds of age, in employment and vocational training. The Equality Bill subsumes but does not change the substance of these provisions.

3.2   There is currently no protection against age discrimination outside employment and vocational training. The Bill prohibits age discrimination in the provision of goods, facilities services and the exercise of public functions.

3.3   Age differs from other protected characteristics in that it is often appropriate for society to treat people differently on grounds of their age. There is also compelling evidence that some age-specific facilities and services will always be needed.

3.4   The Equality Bill prohibits age discrimination against people aged 18 or over. Implementation of the ban will be phased so that service providers have time to address the practical and organisational issues that are likely to arise. As the ban is commenced, the specifics of the new law, in particular the exceptions applicable, will be set out in secondary legislation to be brought forward at the same time.

3.5　　The secondary legislation will include specific exceptions to ensure that different age-based treatment which is beneficial or justifiable can continue in the public and private sectors. A consultation was undertaken from 29 June 2009 to 30 September 2009. Following analysis of the responses the draft secondary legislation will be developed, which will be consulted on in 2010. The aim is for legislation prohibiting age discrimination in services and functions to come into force in 2012.

3.6　　Where a particular differential treatment is based on age and is not covered by a general or specific exception and is then challenged, the Bill provides service providers with an 'objective justification' defence. Under this defence, the practice could continue if it can be shown to represent a 'proportionate means of achieving a legitimate aim'. Objective justification provides a further mechanism for protecting beneficial or justified age-based differences in treatment and is already available to employers under the Equality Employment (Age) Regulations.

Stakeholder engagement

3.7　　Around 80 percent of nearly 750 responses on this issue were in favour of legislation to tackle age discrimination in the provision of goods, facilities and services and the exercise of public functions. The responses included 500 individual responses forwarded by Help the Aged, the vast majority of which supported legislation. At the same time, there were concerns from business and some public sector service providers about the possible impact legislation might have and the potential burdens of complying with the legislation.

3.8   Age equality groups cited a survey[21] which found that almost 30 per cent of adults surveyed reported experiencing age discrimination – more than any other form of prejudice. The Trades Union Congress quoted a Social Exclusion Unit finding[22] that 29 per cent of people over 80 are excluded from important basic services.

3.9   During development of the policy the Treasury also established a working group of financial services and age equality experts (the Financial Services Experts Working Group) to gather and present evidence of the implications and impacts of legislation making age discrimination unlawful in financial services. This Group reported in October 2008. The report does not represent a consensus view, or the view of the Government. The report is available on the HM Treasury website.[23]

3.10   The Government subsequently also commissioned Oxera Consulting Ltd to undertake independent research into how age is used in motor and travel insurance and personal loans. The research was undertaken between February and April 2009. The report is available on the Government Equalities Office website.[24]

---

[21] Age Concern, "How Ageist is Britain?" (2005)

[22] Social Exclusion Unit, "A sure start in later life" (2006)

[23] http://www.hm-treasury.gov.uk/d/age_discrimination.pdf

[24] http://www.equalities.gov.uk/pdf/The%20use%20of%20age-based%20practices%20in%20financial%20services%20Final%20report.pdf

3.11   In April 2009, the then Secretary of State for Health, Alan Johnson, announced a review into the practical action that is needed to tackle age discrimination in health and social care. A national review was undertaken by the Strategic Health Authority, social care bodies and a range of local partners in the South West, which reported to the Secretary of State in October 2009, and included recommendations on the timing of implementation and on those areas of age-based differentiation that should be maintained.

3.12   The Government has continued to consult with children and their representatives on the issues that affect them. For example, in August 2007, the Children's Rights Alliance for England was commissioned to run a dedicated consultation event for children. Some attendees were later invited to meet directly with Ministers. More recently, Government Equalities Office officials have met with 11 Million, the Children's Commissioner for England, the Scottish Commissioner for Children and Young People, and the Children's Rights Alliance for England to discuss how best to address their concerns.

General impact
3.13   In general terms, the legislation will benefit adults of all ages in all protected groups.

Impact on older people

3.14   Tackling age discrimination against older people is especially important in the context of rapid demographic change. Today, people aged over 50 make up one third of the population. By 2021 this will have increased to 40%. The number of 85-year-olds is projected to double within the next 20 years.

3.15   The ban on discrimination is intended to catch only those actions or omissions that result in genuinely unfair discrimination because of age.

3.16   The legislation will not outlaw justifiably different treatment (e.g. free TV licences for over 75s; free bus passes), or treatment which has the effect of counteracting the disadvantages certain age groups face (e.g., travel discounts for age groups likely to be on lower incomes). Consequently, there should be no adverse effects on people who currently benefit from these policies.

3.17   Exceptions to the prohibition will be set out in secondary legislation to be made under the Equality Bill.

Impact on younger people

3.17   The protection will apply to people aged 18 and over. The Government has considered the arguments which were put forward for prohibiting age discrimination against people under the age of 18, but remains unconvinced that discrimination legislation is the most suitable way of meeting children's needs.

3.18   This is because it is almost always right to treat children of different ages in a way which is appropriate to their particular stage of development.

3.19   Any such legislation applying an age discrimination ban to children would require a large number of exceptions to ensure, for example, that a child of a particular age could not insist on the same treatment as an older child or adult, or an adult claim the same treatment as a child. Even with numerous exceptions in place, the risk of unintended consequences and a 'chilling effect' would be high. For example, certain age-based services for children could be withdrawn by service providers in the mistaken belief that they were no longer lawful; or the law might be used as a convenient excuse to withdraw services that would have been withdrawn anyway.

3.20   The Government therefore considers that the practical difficulties of extending protection to under-18s would outweigh the benefits or positive impacts of a general prohibition.

Chapter 4:

Disability-specific changes

4.1   The changes listed below are specifically concerned with equality provisions for disabled people, and will have negligible impact on any of the other equality strands, either individually or collectively. Our discussion of each proposal therefore assesses the impact for disability only.

Disability-related discrimination and indirect disability discrimination

4.2   The Government considered whether it should adopt the principle of indirect discrimination for disability following the House of Lords' judgment in *London Borough of Lewisham v Malcolm* which made it more difficult for a disabled person to establish a case of disability-related discrimination.

4.3   The aim is to re-establish an appropriate balance between the rights of disabled people and those with duties under disability discrimination legislation. Consequently, following consultation with stakeholders, the Government has adopted a revised form of disability-related discrimination in addition to the standard form of indirect discrimination, as currently applied in respect of other protected characteristics, for disability.

Impact on disability

4.4   This will have the effect of restoring disabled people's rights to a position similar to that which existed prior to the

Malcolm judgment, thereby assisting to eliminate unlawful discrimination and promoting equality of opportunity for disabled people. It will also help future-proof the domestic legislation against potential EU developments including the draft EU Anti-Discrimination Directive currently under negotiation, which introduces the concept of indirect discrimination in respect of disability.

Definition of disability

4.5 The Disability Discrimination Act 1995 generally defines a disabled person as someone with a mental or physical impairment which has a substantial and long-term adverse effect on their ability to carry out normal day-to-day activities. In addition, the Act currently requires that the adversely affected day-to-day activities must involve one or more of a list of "capacities", which include mobility, manual dexterity, speech, hearing and eyesight.

4.6 The Equality Bill removes this list of "capacities". This simplifies the way in which the definition of disability operates in relation to "normal day-to-day activities", making the law easier to understand and apply.

Stakeholder engagement

4.7 Around 85% of a total of almost 160 consultation responses on this subject were in favour of this proposal. Commonly, responses mentioned the difficulties that people with mental health or short-term but recurrent conditions had experienced in showing how their impairment impacted on one of the capacities.

Impact on disability

4.8   This measure simplifies the definition of disability and removes the difficulty some disabled people experience in demonstrating that an adversely affected day-to-day activity involves any of the "capacities".

Definition of discrimination

4.9   The Equality Bill replaces the separate definitions of discrimination currently contained in of the Disability Discrimination Act 1995 with a single definition of disability discrimination for rights of access beyond the employment field, without diminishing the legal protection which disabled people have under the current law.

Stakeholder engagement

4.10   Around 75% of a total of more than 180 responses received on this subject were in favour of the proposal.

Impact on disability

4.11   This harmonisation makes the provisions simpler to understand and apply, making it easier for disabled people to understand their rights and helping service providers to meet their responsibilities to disabled people.

Justifications

4.12   The Equality Bill replaces the different justification tests in disability anti-discrimination law with a single objective justification test. It has always been possible to justify certain forms of discrimination under all of the anti-discrimination strands, subject to the terms of the legislation. The standard test for justifying what would otherwise be considered to be indirect discrimination under the other strands is one of "objective justification" which requires that the conduct in question is "a proportionate means of achieving a legitimate aim". The legitimate aim itself must also not be discriminatory in nature. This is not an easy test to satisfy. However there is a considerable body of both domestic and European case law (arising from the jurisprudence of the European Court of Justice) which means that the test is familiar and well understood.[25]

4.13   The Disability Discrimination Act 1995 provides protection from less favourable treatment which occurs for a reason related to the disabled person's disability. As noted above, disability related discrimination will continue in a slightly revised form in the Bill and the concept of indirect discrimination will also be introduced for disability. While the principle of justification exists for disability related discrimination, the legal tests of justification currently differ, depending on the area of activity covered. The Government considers that the time is right to introduce the objective justification test for disability anti-discrimination law.

---

[25] Paragraph 1.35 covers the extension of indirect discrimination to disability.

Stakeholder engagement

4.14   Around 85% of nearly 150 responses received were in favour of the proposal on justifications.

Impact on disability

4.15   This will make the law easier to understand by rationalising the various existing justifications according to the principle of objective justification which applies in other anti-discrimination law. Whilst this will widen the range of circumstances where it will be possible to justify discrimination, the new test will be much more stringent. This will maintain an appropriate balance between the rights of disabled people and the responsibilities of employers and service providers.

The duty to make reasonable adjustments: threshold

4.16   The duty to make adjustments is one of the cornerstones of the Disability Discrimination Act. However, the circumstances in which the duty arises, also known as the "threshold", differs according to which area of life is concerned.

- The duty in relation to the provision of goods, facilities and services etc. is triggered when a policy, practice or procedure or a physical feature makes it "impossible or unreasonably difficult" for a disabled person to access the 'service' in question.

- The duty in relation to the employment field is considered to be a lower "threshold", and is triggered when a provision, criterion or practice, or a physical feature of premises places a disabled person at a "substantial disadvantage" in comparison with persons who are not disabled. (Substantial in this context means something which is more than minor or trivial[26])

4.17   These differing triggers add to the complexity of the law.

4.18   The Equality Bill will therefore introduce a single threshold for the point at which the duty to make adjustments is triggered, based on the lower threshold described above, namely, the "substantial disadvantage" test.

Stakeholder engagement

4.19   Over 80% of around 170 responses received were in favour of this proposal, including the majority of private sector organisations who responded.

Impact on disability

4.20   This proposal will improve consistency and make it clearer for disabled people, employers and service providers to understand their rights and responsibilities under the legislation.

Improving access to and use of premises for disabled people

4.21   The Equality Bill creates a duty on landlords and managers of premises to make disability-related alterations to the common parts of residential premises,

---

[26] Code of Practice: Employment and Occupation (2004), paragraph 5(4)

where reasonable and when requested by a disabled tenant or occupier. This will apply where the disabled person is placed at a substantial disadvantage compared to a non-disabled person. Failure to comply with the duty will be treated as discrimination.

Stakeholder engagement

4.22   Over 90% of more than 150 responses were in favour of this proposal. Respondents who supported the proposal included disability groups, local authorities and public service providers. The main benefit identified by most respondents was lowering the risk of disabled people being isolated in their homes.

Impact on disability

4.23   Some disabled people can become confined to their own homes because they cannot cross the common parts of the premises. This proposal will increase disabled people's independence by allowing them to request and have disability-related alterations made to the common parts where reasonable.

Limiting the use of pre-employment disability-related enquiries

4.24   The Equality Bill includes a provision which limits the use of pre-employment disability-related enquiries to after an applicant has been given the opportunity to demonstrate his suitability for the post except in specified circumstances:

- To identify the need for reasonable adjustments to the recruitment process

- To facilitate diversity monitoring of job applications

- To deliver positive action

- To facilitate employment where a genuine occupational requirement applies in relation to disability.

Stakeholder engagement

4.25   The provision was introduced in response to evidence presented by stakeholders to the Equality Bill Committee in the Commons that pre-employment disability-related enquiries were being used to discriminate against disabled people in the early stages of recruitment, and that such enquiries had a deterrent effect on some disabled people making applications for jobs. The provision was developed following discussion with disability and business organisations, including the Disability Charities Consortium, the Confederation of British Industry, and the Federation of Small Businesses,

Impact on disability

4.26   The limitation on the use of pre-employment disability-related enquiries will reduce opportunities for disability discrimination during the recruitment process and will help to overcome the disincentive effect that disability-related enquiries can have on disabled people applying for jobs, thus increasing their opportunities to participate in the labour market. The provision is expected to have a particular beneficial effect on people aged 16 to 64 who are most likely to be candidates for employment. Restricting the use of disability-related enquiries will also reduce opportunities for discrimination based on dual characteristics, where one characteristic is disability.

Accessible transport

4.27   The Equality Bill is the next step in the process of removing barriers to transport that some members of society still experience. The provisions of Part 12 of the Bill (Disabled persons: transport) have been carried over from existing provisions in the Disability Discrimination Act 1995 which enable regulations to be made requiring taxis, trains, buses, coaches etc to be made accessible to disabled people.

4.28   Regulations requiring all new trains to be accessible were introduced in 1998 and there are already over 4,900 accessible rail vehicles in service. Provisions for buses and coaches were introduced in 2000 and over half of the fleet is already compliant. Appropriate end dates, the latest of which is 1 January 2020, have also been set by which time all train, bus and coach vehicles must be fully compliant.

Stakeholder engagement

4.29   The Department for Transport consulted between January and April 2009 on the issue of improving access for disabled people to taxis. Regulations making taxis more accessible have not yet been used, due to the complex technical and cost issues involved. The Department for Transport is due to publish a strategy for improving access to taxis in late 2009.

4.30 The Department for Transport has also recently completed a consultation on proposals to amend the rail vehicle accessibility regime. New European standards introduced in July 2008 and covering the accessibility of passenger rail vehicles in service on the mainline rail system have prompted a re-assessment of the domestic regime which now covers only light rail vehicles (those used on metro, underground and tram services and prescribed guided modes of transport). The Bill has been drafted to reflect the existing legislation so as not to pre-empt the outcome of this consultation. The Government reserves its position on these issues until it has completed an analysis of the responses to this exercise.

Impact on disability

4.31 The provision of an accessible public transport system in which disabled people can have the same opportunities to travel as other members of society is a key driver in improving their life chances and promoting social inclusion. Without accessible public transport, disabled people may be limited in their ability to access work, visit friends and family, participate in leisure activities or access healthcare and education facilities.

4.32 These changes that have been made to trains, buses and coaches, together with associated improvements in the accessibility of transport infrastructure, are enabling substantial social inclusion benefits to be realised. For example, although disability is not synonymous with age, two thirds of disabled people are older. The provision of accessible public transport will enable people to remain economically active for longer. These provisions will become increasingly important given our aging population.

4.33   The Government does not believe that these provisions will have any differential impact on equality beyond disability although, in making provisions to meet the needs of disabled people, it is noted that the accessibility of public transport vehicles will be improved for all other passengers.

Chapter 5:

Dual discrimination

5.1   The Government wants the law to provide appropriate
        protection against the harmful discrimination people
        actually experience. Currently, the law does not always
        provide a remedy for an individual who experiences
        discrimination because of a combination of protected
        characteristics. In these circumstances, the person
        experiencing such discrimination has to bring separate
        claims in respect of each protected characteristic, such as
        his or her race or sex. However, this can cause problems
        in practice because it can be difficult, complicated and
        sometimes even impossible, to prove such claims.
        Moreover, they do not reflect the discrimination which
        actually occurred.

5.2   For example, a black woman passed over for promotion
        by her employer because she is a black woman would
        have to bring separate claims of discrimination because of
        race and sex. However, she may not succeed in either
        claim if her employer can show that black men and white
        women are not discriminated against and therefore her
        treatment was not because of race or sex alone.

5.3   The Government recognises that people's experience of
        discrimination cannot always be separated into different
        protected characteristics and can be compounded by a
        combination of characteristics. By prohibiting dual

discrimination in the Bill, the intention is to close the gap in existing legislation, providing protection for those who experience this type of discrimination but may otherwise be unable to receive redress or protection under law.

5.4 The provision included in the Equality Bill prohibits discrimination because of a combination of two of the following protected characteristics:

- Age
- Disability
- Gender reassignment
- Race
- Religion or belief
- Sex
- Sexual orientation

5.5 This legislation will have a positive impact for all those in the protected groups and who are treated less favourably because of a combination of their particular characteristics.

5.6 Research conducted by the Citizens Advice Bureaux identified 52 cases in one year that might have qualified for treatment as dual discrimination cases, had the legislation been in place earlier. In these 52, 15 different combinations of characteristics were reported. 88 % involved two of the protected characteristics; and 12% involved three or more of the protected characteristics. We consider those involving 3 or more protected characteristics would be separated out and brought as dual discrimination claims under this provision.

5.7A   By limiting the protected characteristics which can be combined to two, the Bill therefore extends protection to the vast majority of those who need it, without placing an undue burden on businesses or making the law unduly complex.

5.7   It is important to note that these new provisions will also mean a change in the way future discrimination cases are brought. This provision will mean that claimants can bring dual discrimination claims simultaneously with single-strand claims. This will benefit claimants who are not always certain about which characteristics led to their less favourable treatment.

5.8   Enabling claims to be brought simultaneously will ensure that courts and tribunals can consider all the evidence and decide which claims have merit. This means that courts and tribunals could find that the person was discriminated against because of either or both the single strands, because of the combination of 2 characteristics or because of all three claims.

Stakeholder engagement and research

5.10   These provisions were developed by the Government Equalities Office following consultation and further discussions with a wide range of government departments and stakeholders including equality representatives, trade unions and business.

5.11 In our Discrimination Law Review consultation document *Framework for Fairness: Proposals for a Single Equality Bill for Great Britain,* published in June 2007, we recognised that many people were concerned that the current law does not adequately protect those who experience multiple discrimination. We therefore asked for evidence about instances of this kind of discrimination and of people having difficulties in securing legal redress in such circumstances to inform our approach.

5.12 There were nearly one hundred responses to the question about multiple discrimination. Generally, there was a large volume of support for additional protection – from equality organisations, trade unions, voluntary bodies and legal organisations. Business respondents were mainly concerned that the law should not be significantly harder for employers to understand and comply with. This has been one of the key issues which we have explored further.

5.14 We developed a proposal enabling claims to be brought combining two protected characteristics, to be implemented in or after April 2011.

5.15 In our 2009 discussion document *Equality Bill: Assessing the impact of a multiple discrimination provision,* we described how we consider this provision would operate in practice. Through this document, we sought views from a wide range of stakeholders, on the potential impact of our proposals. During the discussion period we held a series of meetings with equality stakeholders, trade unions, the public sector, employers and business representatives. We received 53 responses. In addition, bilateral meetings were held with key business stakeholders.

5.16   In addition, research was commissioned in the form of a study of discrimination cases handled by the Citizens Advice Bureaux. The purpose of the research was to ascertain the extent and nature of multiple discrimination and to assess the number and type of protected characteristics most commonly involved.

5.17   In the light of the feedback received from the discussions and analysis of the research we commissioned, we decided to introduce a provision for dual discrimination as part of the Equality Bill currently being considered by Parliament. The corresponding amendment was agreed during the Committee stage of the Bill.

General impact

5.18   This provision will help individuals with protected characteristics by providing protection against discrimination where it is currently difficult and sometimes impossible to get a legal remedy.

5.19   The implementation date of April 2011 (six months after the planned implementation of most of the Bill's provisions in October 2010) will have an impact generally. The negative impact is that those experiencing dual discrimination will be waiting longer for redress. However, the positive impact will be that more time can be dedicated to producing and understanding guidance as well as adjusting behaviour and perceptions as necessary so that protection is more effective.

Impact on race

5.20   Our evidence shows that a dual discrimination provision is likely to have a significant positive impact on race equality and that the majority of incidents of discrimination because of a combination of characteristics involve race. For example, the CAB research identified that 86% of the cases presented involved race combined with one or more other protected characteristics. Such individuals will be able to seek redress if they are discriminated against because of the combination of their race and another relevant, protected characteristic.

Impact on age

5.21   The CAB research identified that age was combined with one or more other protected characteristics in 14% of the cases presented. This means that such individuals will be able to rely on this provision if they are discriminated against because of the combination of their age and another relevant, protected characteristic.

Impact on sex

5.22   The CAB research identified that sex was combined with one or more other protected characteristics in 45% of the cases presented. This indicates that a significant number of incidents involve a person's sex. This means that where an individual is discriminated against because of their sex combined with another relevant, protected characteristic, they will be able to seek redress.

Impact on religion or belief

5.23   The discrimination cases identified by the CAB research which involved religion and belief always involved race as well and were specific to people who are Asian and Muslim. Religion or belief was involved in 34% of the cases presented for the CAB research. A dual discrimination provision will therefore have a positive impact on these groups in particular. This means therefore that there will be a significant impact for these groups who will now be able to rely on this provision when they experience discrimination because of the combination of their religion or belief and another relevant, protected characteristic.

Impact on disability

5.24   The research identified that 43% of the cases presented involved disability combined with one or more other protected characteristics. This evidence suggests that a number of incidents involve disability. This means that such individuals will be able to rely on this provision if they are discriminated against because of the combination of their disability and another relevant, protected characteristic.

Impact on sexual orientation

5.25 We consider that there may be some under-reporting of incidents involving sexual orientation and whilst sexual orientation does not seem to feature as prominently as other characteristics in incidents of multiple discrimination, it is possible that in some cases a single-strand remedy is inadequate. Therefore its inclusion will have a positive impact for those people who will be able to seek redress where they are discriminated against because of their sexual orientation combined with another protected characteristic.

Impact on gender reassignment

5.26 As is the position with sexual orientation, we consider that there may be under-reporting of incidents involving gender reassignment and whilst gender reassignment does not seem to feature as prominently as other characteristics in incidents of multiple discrimination, we think that in some cases a single-strand remedy is inadequate. Therefore its inclusion will have a positive impact for those people who will be able to seek redress where they are discriminated against because of their gender reassignment combined with another relevant, protected characteristic.

Impact on victimisation protection

5.27 As protection from victimisation concerns someone who has made, or assisted in making, a claim under the legislation rather than in relation to any particular protected characteristic, it follows that victimisation protection will be available for those involved in dual discrimination claims as it is with a single-strand claim. Claims based on combined grounds will be treated in the same manner as single-strand claims when assessed for good faith for the purpose of subsequent victimisation claims. Where single-strand claims are brought alongside dual discrimination claims it would be for the tribunal or court to determine which allegation resulted in the alleged detriment. This will therefore benefit those individuals who may face victimisation which is linked to their dual discrimination claim.

<u>Areas not impacted by these provisions</u>

5.28   As **pregnancy and maternity** do not require a comparator for single strand claims, it is difficult to see how pregnancy and maternity could be combined in a dual discrimination claim with other characteristics which do require a comparator without risking reintroduction of a comparator to the pregnancy and maternity strand. This would mean that whilst there cannot be a comparator for single-strand claims of discrimination because of pregnancy and maternity, a comparator would be required for a dual discrimination claim involving pregnancy and maternity. The complexities that this could create are disproportionate in light of the lack of evidence that extending the coverage of dual discrimination claims across pregnancy and maternity is necessary to remedy unlawful discrimination. A claimant alleging discrimination because of pregnancy and maternity need only show that it was an effective cause of the less favourable treatment. This means that claims involving pregnancy and maternity are likely to succeed on a single-strand basis and therefore exclusion from dual discrimination claims will not negatively impact equality in this respect.

5.29   It is considered that it is not necessary to include **marriage and civil partnerships** as such claims are likely to succeed on a sex or sexual orientation basis respectively in any case. As with pregnancy and maternity, there is a lack of evidence that extending protection to cover marriage and civil partnerships is required.

5.30   There has been no evidence provided to suggest that **harassment** cases are failing due to a lack of an intersectional remedy as provided against dual discrimination. The broader definition of harassment in the Bill (replacing the test of conduct "on grounds of" a protected characteristic with one of conduct "related to" a protected characteristic) makes it even less likely that intersectional harassment would fail to find a remedy by means of a single-strand claim. It is therefore considered that there is no need to cover harassment within the dual discrimination provisions and its exclusion should not have a negative impact on equality.

5.31   We are not convinced of a need to enable dual discrimination claims to include **indirect discrimination** as there is little evidence of indirect discrimination claims failing which would otherwise succeed when based on a combination of protected characteristics. For example, dress codes preventing Muslim women from wearing veils or Sikh men from wearing turbans could be remedied under current law. As there is limited evidence that the single-strand approach does not work in respect of indirect discrimination, its exclusion should not have a negative impact on equality.

Chapter 6:

Extending harassment protection

Employer liability for third party harassment at work

6.1   The Bill extends employer liability for third party harassment of their employees in the workplace to race, disability, sexual orientation, religion or belief and age. Such protection already exists against sex harassment, sexual harassment and harassment on grounds of gender reassignment.

General impact

6.2   Extending employer liability for third party harassment of their employees by third parties such as customers or suppliers provides a consistent level of protection for employees across the protected grounds of sex, gender reassignment, race, disability, sexual orientation, religion or belief and age. So if an employee were to be subjected repeatedly to third party harassment on any of these protected grounds, and if the employer knew this was happening and failed to take reasonable steps to stop it happening again, the employee would be able to bring a claim against the employer.

6.3   This measure will reduce confusion for employers and their employees about their respective responsibilities and rights in this respect and make it clear that employees have the same rights in this respect for all the protected characteristics.

Harassment outside the workplace

6.4   The Equality Bill also extends protection against harassment outside the workplace to age and disability where currently there is no protection, and provide comprehensive protection for race, sex and gender reassignment where existing protection applies on a piecemeal basis

Impact on race, sex and gender reassignment

6.5   Freestanding statutory protection against harassment outside the workplace already exists for race (including ethnic or national origin but not colour or nationality), sex and gender reassignment in the provision of goods, facilities or services and management or disposal of premises; for race (including ethnic or national origin, but not colour or nationality) and sex in the exercise of public functions (though for race, only in respect of certain public functions); and for race (again, not including colour or nationality) in education in schools. The Bill will extend this protection for colour and nationality to the provision of goods, facilities or services, management or disposal of premises and education in schools; for sex to education in schools; for gender reassignment to the exercise of public functions; for race (including ethnic or national origin, colour and nationality) to the exercise of all public functions; and to all three grounds in relation to associations. (See Chapter 11 on 'Private clubs and associations').

Impact on age and disability

6.6   There is currently no legislation against age discrimination outside the workplace. Extending protection against harassment outside the workplace to cover age has the potential to strengthen protection from degrading treatment when accessing services provided for particular age groups, for example in residential care settings. Similar benefits will apply to disabled people.

Impact on sexual orientation and religion or belief

6.7   The Bill will maintain the existing provisions which do not cover protection against harassment because of sexual orientation and religion or belief outside the workplace. Therefore there will be no additional impact on these strands.

6.8   It is considered that examples of harassment under these strands which respondents to the consultation provided would either fall outside the scope of the Bill, for example physical or verbal attacks in the street, or would potentially be caught by discrimination provisions.

Chapter 7:

Public functions and goods, facilities and services

7.1   The Equality Bill takes a harmonised approach to the way
        the law treats the exercise of public functions and the
        provision of goods, facilities and services, across all
        protected grounds.

7.2   It also extends the coverage of the public functions
        provisions to provide protection for gender reassignment,
        pregnancy and maternity and age (for those aged 18 or
        over)[27], to ensure consistent coverage across all the
        strands[28].

Background

7.3   Domestic discrimination law protects people from
        discrimination in broad areas of activity including the
        supply of goods, facilities and services and the exercise of
        public functions.

7.4   The term "goods, facilities and services" covers a very
        wide range of provision to the public or a section of the
        public by public, private and voluntary sector
        organisations. It does not matter whether someone is
        asked to pay or not. Existing legislation gives illustrative
        examples of facilities and services. These include
        accommodation in a hotel and facilities for transport and

---

[27] The public functions provisions will only be extended to cover age when the power taken in
the Bill to prohibit age discrimination outside the employment areas is exercised.
[28] This does not include marriage and civil partnership.

travel. Also included in the illustrative examples for race, sex and disability are the services of local and public authorities. This would cover activities ranging from the provision of local authority-run libraries or leisure facilities to the provision of information by Her Majesty's Revenue and Customs on how to apply for tax benefits.

7.5   The public functions provisions are more recent additions to the discrimination legislation. Currently, discrimination in the exercise of public functions is unlawful on the grounds of race, disability, sex, religion or belief and sexual orientation. These provisions were introduced to ensure that all the activities of those exercising a public function were subject to the prohibition on discrimination, not simply activities that were considered to involve the provision of facilities and services.

Stakeholder engagement

7.6   During the consultation we asked respondents whether they agreed that there would be benefits in adopting a harmonised approach to the way the law treats the exercise of public functions and the provision of goods, facilities and services, across all protected strands. We received 195 responses of which 96% were in favour of the Government's proposal to adopt a harmonised approach.

7.7   Overall, equality stakeholders endorsed the harmonisation of what they consider to be an inaccessible and inconsistent law, which makes it difficult for individuals to understand their rights. No group of equality stakeholders raised strong opposition to this measure at any stage.

<u>General impact</u>

7.8   Currently different pieces of discrimination legislation contain differences in the interaction between the provisions on goods, facilities and services and those relating to public functions. The legislation reflects the same policy intention: to ensure that all the activities of bodies carrying out public functions are subject to the prohibition on discrimination unless expressly excepted.

7.9   Adopting a harmonised approach to the way the law treats public functions and goods, facilities and services provisions across all protected grounds will give greater certainty. It will make it easier for customers to know their rights and easier for service providers to know their responsibilities, as the same rules will apply to all of the discrimination strands of race, sex, disability, religion or belief, age, gender reassignment, pregnancy and maternity and sexual orientation. The biggest benefit, however, will be for the strands that do not currently have protection from discrimination in public functions. This includes protection from discrimination because of gender reassignment, explicit protection for women who are pregnant or new mothers and protection because of age (for over 18s).

Impact on gender reassignment

7.10   The obligations of bodies carrying out public functions in relation to people who are proposing to undergo, are undergoing or have undergone gender reassignment will be consistent with their existing obligations towards other groups.

7.11   This will lead to a fairer outcome for transsexual people who otherwise would not have the same degree of protection.

Impact on gender (pregnancy and maternity)

7.12   The public functions provisions in the Sex Discrimination Act 1975 already apply in relation to sex. As public authorities already have public functions obligations in relation to men and women, it is likely that they already take into account pregnant women and new mothers, so there may be little noticeable impact on this strand, but any impact will be positive.

7.13   Nevertheless, extending the public function provisions to cover pregnancy and maternity will make it explicit that the obligations of bodies carrying out public functions in relation to pregnant women and new mothers are consistent with their obligations towards other groups, thereby eliminating potentially confusing inconsistencies in the law and making it easier for authorities to provide guidance and training for staff.

7.14   The pregnancy and maternity provisions will not provide protection in relation to education in schools. The Government considers that there are already sufficient legal duties on schools to ensure the wellbeing of individual pupils, including schoolgirls who are pregnant or new mothers. In addition, the needs of these pupils, who must be enabled to continue their education while taking into account their particular needs, are best considered on a case by case basis (e.g. home tuition where this is the girl's preference) rather than treating them in exactly the same way as other pupils.

Impact on age

7.15   The impact of extending protection against age discrimination in the provision of goods, facilities and services and the exercise of public functions is described at Chapter 3 – 'Protecting against age discrimination outside the workplace'.

Chapter 8:

Updating equal pay provisions

8.1 Currently domestic law on pay-related discrimination between women and men is covered by two separate Acts; the Sex Discrimination Act and the Equal Pay Act. The Equal Pay Act deals with contractual pay (and matters such as bonuses or other entitlements where they are contractual). Under the contractual approach, it is unlawful for employers to pay male and female employees doing like work, work rated as equivalent or work of equal value differently, unless there is a genuine difference in circumstances which is unrelated to gender.

8.2 The Equality Bill:

- retains the separate approaches for contractual and non-contractual pay and other matters;

- simplifies the equal pay legislation to make it easier for it to work in practice and clarify the way the burden of proof and "genuine material factor" defence operate.

Stakeholder engagement

8.3 We have had ongoing meetings with equality stakeholders since the consultation, including the Equality and Human Rights Commission and the Fawcett Society.

8.4 A significant majority of respondents to the 2007 consultation paper were in favour of retaining the separate approach between contractual and non-contractual pay, although some argued against this approach because of the length and complexity of equal pay cases. There was no clear agreement on codification of existing case-law in the response to the consultation, with the benefits both of the flexibility of case-law and of increased clarity being recognised.

Impact on gender

8.5   It is accepted that having two approaches (for contractual and non-contractual pay) covering pay-related sex discrimination adds a level of complexity. However, maintaining consistency with the current position will maintain the benefit of the specific contractual right to equality, which for the most part benefits women. It will also maximise the relevance and advantages of the developing body of case-law, and will avoid the potential for considerable confusion that could be generated by a switch to some other approach.

8.6   Clarifying the law will help both claimants and employers know what their position is and what employees' rights are. Again this will primarily benefit women.

8.7   In combination with other transparency measures (see also Chapter 9) being taken forward by the Government, the Equality Bill will encourage the adoption and implementation by employers of good pay policies and practices, which ensure that jobs are evaluated and rewarded fairly, and this will reduce the risk of discrimination and inequality.

General impact

8.8   The Bill's equal pay provisions will benefit women and
        men across all the protected characteristics, so people of
        all protected characteristics will therefore be protected
        from pay discrimination because of sex.

Chapter 9:

Transparency: banning 'pay secrecy clauses' in employees' contracts of employment; gender pay gap publication power

9.1   The Equality Bill makes 'pay secrecy clauses' unenforceable so that colleagues can discuss their pay and challenge employers who unlawfully pay them less. It will protect employees against victimisation by the employer where they discuss their pay in breach of any such clause. It also provides a power to require private sector employers with at least 250 employees to publish their gender pay gap. The intention is to use this power from 2013 if sufficient progress on voluntary reporting is not made by then. The Equality and Human Rights Commission is consulting on proposals for such voluntary reporting.

Stakeholder engagement

9.2   While these issues were not covered in the main, formal consultation, a number of responses to the consultation on the Bill made proposals regarding 'pay secrecy clauses'.

9.3   On gender pay gap reporting, separate discussions with business and other stakeholders suggested that businesses were not generally opposed in principle to publishing gender pay information, nor was this expected to require much in the way of additional data collection or processing. However, some stakeholders felt strongly that companies would not want to limit any reporting to a single figure (which by itself could be misleading) but would need to include a narrative report or other context around it for proper explanation.

9.4 Equality and union stakeholders were generally in favour of the proposal, though in some cases this needed to be seen in the context of demands to go further – for example, by making equal pay audits or reviews mandatory.

9.5 Both business and union stakeholders are currently working with the Equality and Human Rights Commission to consult on and produce a set of measurements that employers can use to voluntarily report on their pay gaps.

Impact on gender
(i) Banning pay secrecy clauses

9.6 Banning secrecy clauses makes pay matters more transparent because employees will feel free to discuss their pay details with colleagues without breaching their contracts of employment.

9.7 In its response to the consultation, the Equal Opportunities Commission cited research[29] carried out for it in 2003 which found that 22 per cent of employers did not allow employees to share information about their pay with their colleagues. It also found that women on lower

---

[29] *Monitoring Progress Towards Pay Equality*

wages were more likely to be unaware of the pay of their peers than higher earners; and that women were also more likely to be unaware of the pay of their colleagues than men were.

9.8   This measure will therefore help women challenge their employer where they find that they are being paid less than their male colleagues doing equal work.

(ii) Gender pay gap reporting

9.9   The power to require gender pay gap reporting serves a similar purpose: transparency. While national data exist on the gender pay gap, there are no such data at employer level. The provision of such information will help identify where problems may potentially exist, against the background of a persistent gender pay gap at national level. This measure will therefore help encourage business to focus on reducing any gender pay gap within their organisation; and will thus benefit women who historically receive lower pay. It may also help potential employees, particularly women, who may find the published information helpful in determining their choice of prospective employer.

General impact

9.10   There will be particular benefit for women in terms of the increased transparency which both measures should encourage, and there will be direct benefit to men who are protected from victimisation if they choose to disclose pay details to women.

Chapter 10:

Extending protection against discrimination because of gender reassignment, to education in schools

10.1   The Equality Bill extends protection against discrimination because of gender reassignment to education in schools.

Stakeholder engagement

10.2   We have met a number of trans groups since publishing the Government response to the consultation. These groups have commented on the problems caused by bullying of gender variant children in school. A report[30] for the Equalities Review by Press for Change, stated that 64% of trans men and 44% of trans women recalled experiencing harassment or bullying at school.

Impact on gender variant children

10.3   In the consultation paper and the Government Response, the Government indicated that it considered it unnecessary to extend protection on grounds of gender reassignment to pupils in schools. The Government has listened to further representations. It also acknowledges that there are a small number of children who live and attend school in the opposite gender to their birth gender. Around 50[31]-60[32] children per annum are referred to the Gender Identity Development Unit at the Tavistock and

---

[30] Engendered Penalties: Transgender and Transsexual People's Experiences of Inequality and Discrimination (http://www.pfc.org.uk/files/EngenderedPenalties.pdf)

[31] http://www.dh.gov.uk/en/Publicationsandstatistics/Publications/PublicationsPolicyAndGuidance/DH_082976

Portman NHS Trust. Such children can experience distress from their gender dysphoria and it is considered right that they should be protected from discrimination and unfair treatment within schools that could only cause further distress. This will also mean gender variant children will receive the same level of protection as gay and lesbian children.

10.4 This extension of protection should lead to a more supportive school environment. The Department for Children, Schools and Families is developing guidance on gender and gender variant bullying.

---

[32] http://www.gires.org.uk/assets/early-medical-treatment.pdf

Chapter 11:

Private clubs and associations

11.1   Currently, discrimination by associations (including private members' clubs) (with 25 or more members) is outlawed on the grounds of race, disability and sexual orientation. Protection is provided to existing and prospective members, associates and prospective associates. Discrimination against guests is also outlawed, but currently only on the grounds of disability.

11.2   The Equality Bill extends protection against discrimination by associations because of sex, religion or belief, gender reassignment, pregnancy and maternity and age. It will also prohibit discrimination against guests and prospective guests on all grounds.

Stakeholder engagement

11.3   The consultation revealed a relatively high level of interest in the proposals – nearly 200 responses of which the great majority (77%) were in favour of extending protection as suggested.

11.4   Religion and belief groups have been the least supportive. Their main concern was that the new legislation will prevent clubs from selectively choosing members who uphold their religious principles. The law will not prevent this and we have addressed this under the section on general impact.

General impact

11.5   A single law based on a single set of principles will make it easier for all associations to understand their responsibilities. Applying the prohibition only to associations with 25 or more members will ensure that the law does not impinge on private gatherings, nor clubs that are open to the public. (In the latter case, the goods, facilities and services provisions, considered in Chapter 7 above, will apply).

11.6   None of the existing or new prohibitions affect or will affect associations that are purely for the benefit of people with shared protected characteristics, *as regards their membership*: i.e. clubs for women; support groups for gay men or lesbians; clubs for people of a particular religion. The provisions will, however, affect associations where there is mixed membership e.g. a private members' club open to both men and women could not treat women less favourably than men.

11.7   In addition, sports clubs will not be forced to allow women to compete alongside men. There is already an exception in law which allows men and women to be treated differently in "any sport, game or other activity of a competitive nature where the physical strength, stamina or physique of the average woman puts her at a disadvantage to the average man."[33] The Government has no plans to remove this provision.

---

[33] Sex Discrimination Act 1975

11.8   Associations will, if they wish, be able to distinguish between the benefits, services and facilities available to members and those available to guests, provided that this is *not* done solely on the basis of a protected characteristic.

Impact on disability

11.9   Current disability legislation already provides for protection for members, potential members, associates and guests, so there will be no additional impact on disability.

Impact on race and sexual orientation

11.10   Race and sexual orientation discrimination legislation on associations does not currently apply to guests. The Equality Bill will extend coverage to protect guests, which will provide clarity and consistency and will benefit people of different racial groups and different sexual orientations. It is difficult to see why it would be acceptable to discriminate against a guest when it would not be acceptable to discriminate against a member.

11.11   Private members' clubs will, if they wish, be able to distinguish between the services and facilities available to members and those available to guests.

Impact on gender, age, pregnancy and maternity and gender reassignment

11.12   The Equality Bill will prohibit discrimination by

associations against members, potential members and associates because of gender, age, gender reassignment and pregnancy and maternity. These strands will have the same or similar protection to that already enjoyed by those protected on grounds of race, sexual orientation and on grounds of disability.

11.13   It is not right for mixed-membership associations to be able to treat some of their members or guests on less favourable terms than others and the consultation response broadly confirms this, with trade union, sexual orientation, race, legal, disability and gender stakeholders unanimous in their support for the proposals.

11.14   This new protection will have a positive impact on all strands. Examples of discrimination because of particular characteristics that will be prohibited include: restricted access to club facilities; reduced membership rights; and being excluded from the club's decision-making processes.

11.15   Protection is also being extended on all grounds to cover guests. This will give the same benefits as listed above for race and sexual orientation.

Impact on religion or belief

11.16   The Equality Bill will also prohibit associations from discriminating because of religion or belief. However, in designing the legislation the Government wishes to avoid inadvertently preventing or hampering the very important work that religious organisations currently do, ranging from specifically religious activities to purely social events that nevertheless bring together members of the same religion or belief.

11.17   In order to avoid such unwanted effects, religious associations which restrict membership to those of only a particular religion can benefit from the specific exception for single-characteristic associations mentioned above. Religious associations can also benefit from a more general exception for religious organisations contained in the legislation which allows them to restrict membership, participation in activities and the provision of services on grounds of religion or belief provided that doing so is due to the purpose of the organisation or to avoid causing offence on grounds of religion or belief.

11.18   Instead, the type of behaviour we are seeking to outlaw is for example, private clubs only scheduling open days on religious holidays or enforcing dress requirements that are incompatible with certain religious doctrines. This could amount to indirect discrimination on the grounds of religion or belief.

11.19   We believe the extension of protection to religion or belief will have a positive impact by ending discriminatory practices that prevent people from fully participating in, or becoming members of, associations and private clubs.

Chapter 12:

Enforcement

Extending the power of tribunals to make recommendations that benefit the wider workforce

12.1   Employment tribunals currently have a power in discrimination cases to make a recommendation that the respondent "take within a specified period action appearing to the tribunal to be practicable for the purpose of obviating or reducing the adverse effect on the complainant of any act of discrimination to which the complaint relates". These recommendations must be made for the benefit of the individual complainant. The Equality Bill extends the recommendation powers so that recommendations can be made for the benefit not only of the individual claimant but also others who may be affected by the act of discrimination.

12.2   The Equality and Human Rights Commission will be notified of any recommendations made by the tribunal and will be able to help employers comply with a recommendation and follow this up using its existing powers, if it considered it appropriate. Where an employer fails to take steps to address the recommendations, there will be no penalty for non-compliance. However, the tribunal will be able to draw inferences from this lack of action in subsequent cases against the employer which involved the same or a similar set of facts.

Stakeholder engagement

12.3   The consultation did not ask explicitly about wider recommendations. However, a significant number of stakeholders provided views on this issue, including the Employers' Forum on Disability which supported tribunals being able to make recommendations even when the employee is no longer employed, so as to effect systemic change. This issue was instead consulted on as part of the Dispute Resolution Review consultation in 2007. Organisations in favour included unions, equality groups and representatives of the Employment Tribunals, though business generally opposed.

General impact

12.4   Allowing a tribunal to make wider recommendations will mean that where a female employee leaves her employer because of discrimination and subsequently wins the case, the tribunal can recommend that the employer should, for example, introduce an equal opportunities policy.

12.5   This will not benefit the woman who has left, but it will have positive impacts on the women still in the workforce. And it will also benefit the employer, who will be less vulnerable to future claims. If the employer does not implement the recommendation and a further claim is made, the tribunal will be able to take the earlier recommendation into account when considering the case.

12.6   Specific examples of cases where tribunals have made wider recommendations to employers:

- Wilkinson –v- Swedecor Ltd (1999): the tribunal found that the company had no effective equal opportunities policy and recommended that one was introduced in line with code of practice.

- Bourne –v- Roberts and The Post Office: the tribunal recommended that the employer should identify a toilet on the premises as "unisex" after a victimisation claim was made by a transgender employee.

12.7   Complying with a recommendation to improve policy or practice will help an employer address systemic problems; this in turn will encourage better employment practice and should help reduce instances of race, sex, disability and other types of discrimination within employment.

12.8   Recommendations are a light-touch, risk-based way of reducing discriminatory practices within organisations and achieving a fairer and more equitable workplace for all, including individuals who belong to each of the equality strands.

12.9   Over time, we would expect that this will impact

positively on all the protected strands. The biggest
positive impact may initially be seen in the areas of
race, sex and disability where most tribunal cases
occur, but it should apply proportionally to all strands
depending on the number of cases brought to tribunals.

Type of Discrimination	Number of successful claims in 2006/07 (taken from ETS Annual Report)
Sex*[34]	463
Race	102
Equal Pay*	126
Age	0
Disability	149
Sexual Orientation	21
Religion or Belief	12
Total	873

Improving the effectiveness of courts and improving access to justice

12.10   A number of measures related to the Bill will help
enhance discrimination expertise in the courts
including:

- A request to the Lord Chief Justice (or designated
Senior Judiciary) and the Judicial Studies Board to
consider whether there are any training implications
arising from the Equality Bill

---

[34] To note: many of the claims marked * related to equal pay/sex discrimination multiple claims brought against the NHS and Local Authorities in Scotland and in England and Wales.

- Providing in the Bill for the use of expert "assessors" (i.e. discrimination experts) to advise judges in cases in the civil courts involving discrimination across all the equality strands.

- Enabling disability discrimination school education cases in Scotland to be heard in the Additional Support Needs Tribunals (Scotland) rather than the sheriff courts where they are heard at present.

12.11   We will look to improve access to justice by:

- Reversing the burden of proof for all discrimination cases, rather than in respect of just some protected characteristics. This means that, if the claimant presents facts from which the court or tribunal could decide, in the absence of any adequate explanation, that there has been direct or indirect discrimination or discrimination arising from disability, it will be for the respondent to prove that there has been no breach of the principle of equal treatment.

Stakeholder engagement

12.12   Equality stakeholders who responded to the consultation were generally in favour of these proposals to increase the courts' expertise and improve access to justice.

General impact

12.13   These proposals should lead to more consistent judgments which in turn should increase confidence in the civil courts' handling of discrimination claims. They will be relatively straightforward to implement and may help to increase the efficiency of hearings, reducing the amount of time actually spent in court. Over time, all the protected strands should benefit proportionately as the courts' familiarity with discrimination cases grows.

12.14 Shifting the burden of proof to the respondent, for cases involving all protected characteristics, once the claimant has established the initial facts of their claim, will also improve access to justice as individuals will find it easier to bring a claim. This is because where a person considers that they have been discriminated against and can provide sufficient evidence of this fact; the onus to prove discrimination has not occurred then falls to the respondent in a court case. For example:

- A man of Chinese ethnic origin applies for a promotion at work but is not given an interview for the job. On investigation he finds that a number of white colleagues were given interviews despite having less experience and fewer qualifications. He brings a case for race discrimination before the tribunal and provides sufficient evidence that would allow the tribunal to presume that discrimination had occurred. It would then be up to his employer to prove why he had not discriminated against him.

Impact on disability

12.15 Over 90% of equality stakeholders supported the

extension of the powers of the Additional Support Needs Tribunals for Scotland to include consideration of disability discrimination cases in education. Stakeholders felt this will have the following positive impacts on disabled people:

- Remedies in Scotland will be brought into line with the broadly equivalent systems in England and Wales;

- Users will experience a more accessible, user-friendly, cheaper system that is able to act more responsively to their needs;

- Users of the system will find it a more appropriate forum for hearing cases relating to education as Additional Support Needs Tribunals know and understand the school context and are experienced in dealing sensitively with cases concerning children and young people with additional support needs.

Chapter 13:

Establishing a single Equality Duty on public authorities; with a power to make specific duties, including in respect of public procurement by some authorities

13.1   The first public sector duty, for race, was introduced in 2001. Similar duties for disability and gender followed in 2006 and 2007.

13.2   The Equality Bill brings together the three existing equality duties on race, disability and gender into a new single Equality Duty, and extends it to cover age (with a limited exception for children in schools), sexual orientation, religion or belief, pregnancy and maternity explicitly and gender re-assignment (which is currently only partly covered by the gender duty).

13.3   The new Equality Duty requires public authorities to "have due regard" to the need to eliminate unlawful discrimination, advance equality of opportunity and foster good relations between people who share a protected characteristic and those who do not.. The Bill provides a power to impose specific duties on public authorities, including in relation to the public procurement functions of certain public authorities ("contracting authorities", within the meaning of the EU Public Sector Directive). This will help ensure purchasing by contracting authorities is used to support the delivery of equality outcomes.

13.4   Proposals for the specific duties are currently being developed according to four principles: use of evidence; consultation and involvement; transparency; and capability. These proposals will be put out to consultation shortly after the Bill is introduced.

Stakeholder engagement

13.5   In February 2007, the Government Equalities Office commissioned research from Schneider-Ross to understand the lessons learnt from implementation of the race duty and how public authorities were seeking to meet the requirements of the gender and disability duties. The research, published in November 2007, showed that over 40% of the respondents had chosen to develop a single equality scheme and over 90% felt that there were benefits of having a single equality scheme.

13.6   In response to the consultation on proposals for the Equality Bill, over 80% favoured combining the current, race, gender and disability duties.   Over 90% supported proposals to extend the duties to cover age, religion or belief, sexual orientation and gender reassignment.

13.7   There have been ongoing discussions with practitioners and key stakeholders. The Government Equalities Office has also commissioned further independent research to assess the impact of the current specific duties. In addition, the Government Equalities Office has set up a stakeholder reference group to advise on the specific duties. An additional consultation on specific duties to underpin the general duty was carried out from June to September 2009.

General impact

13.8   Examples of how the existing duties have helped make a real difference, include:

- a police authority introducing an emergency mobile phone text service for deaf people;

- a local council introducing new, accessible, public toilets for disabled people;

- health authorities understanding that men are less likely to visit GPs than women, and so targeting men in other environments, such as barber shops or football matches;

- a local authority establishing a rapid response team to deal with racial conflicts quickly and in a culturally-sensitive way.

13.9   The Government is keen for initiatives like these to continue, and for their benefits to extend to the new strands. The Duty will deliver positive benefits for people of different ages, sexual orientations, religious beliefs (including those with no religious belief) and people undergoing or who have undergone gender reassignment, because it will provide a legislative imperative which encourages public authorities to consider the impact of their policies on these new strands, as well as the strands covered by the existing duties.

Impact on age

13.10   Including age within the new Equality Duty will require public authorities to consider how to eliminate discrimination, advance equality of opportunity and foster good relations for people of different ages.

13.11   The Duty will not require schools to promote equality of opportunity for children of different ages. It is not considered that this will have an adverse impact on equality for children as there is no evidence that a requirement to promote equality of opportunity between, for example, 12 and 13 year olds is needed. Further, such a duty would not make sense in an environment that is built on treating children of different ages differently.

13.12   Including age within the new Equality Duty might mean:

For older people:

- a council might decide to provide extra park benches in local parks, so that older people can benefit from public spaces as well as younger people;

- a local authority might conclude that a kerb-side refuse collection is not suitable for some old people, and introduce an "assisted lift" scheme to help older people who are unable to wheel their bins round to the front of their houses;

- a library might provide IT training specifically for older people.

For children (outside schools):

- local authorities might make sure swimming pools and leisure centres are accessible for children as well as adults;

- local councils might make changes so that their bus services cater better for children.

Impact on religion or belief

13.13   Including religion or belief in the new Equality Duty will require public authorities to consider how to eliminate discrimination, advance equality of opportunity and foster good relations for people of different religions or beliefs. This could result in health and social care providers analysing different levels of use of their services between different communities and taking positive steps to ensure access to services and better outcomes. This might, for example, particularly help Muslim women of Bangladeshi and Pakistani origin who have significantly poorer maternal and child health outcomes and are significantly less likely to access ante-natal services, partly because they are concerned they will be unable to receive services from women.

13.14 However, the duty is geared towards the religion or belief of individuals in the community. It is not directed toward the promotion of particular religions or beliefs.

Impact on sexual orientation

13.15 Including sexual orientation in the new Equality Duty will require public authorities to consider how to eliminate discrimination, advance equality of opportunity and foster good relations for people of different sexual orientations.

13.16 This could lead, for example, to some care homes reconsidering their staff training, to ensure staff are sensitive and responsive to the needs of older gay people.

Impact on the existing duties (race, gender, disability)

13.17 Some equality stakeholders have expressed concern that the existing duties could be "diluted" by being integrated in a single Equality Duty. They believe that public authorities might think an expanded duty means less attention needs to be paid to disabled people, for example, and their needs. This is not the case; the new Duty will require public authorities to have "due regard" to the three elements of the duty (eliminate discrimination; advance equality; foster good relations) in respect of each of the protected characteristics. It will not weaken the impact of the existing duties, since their effect is replicated in the new Duty.

Impact on race

13.18   The current race equality duty requires public authorities to have due regard to the need to eliminate racial discrimination, to promote equality of opportunity for persons of different racial groups and to promote good race relations. The new Equality Duty will replicate these elements. It will also make clear that "advancing equality of opportunity" includes, in particular, overcoming or minimising disadvantages suffered by certain racial groups and meeting their different needs. This should encourage public authorities to take a more proactive approach to achieving equality for people of different racial groups.

Impact on gender

13.19   The current gender equality duty requires public authorities to eliminate unlawful discrimination and harassment and to promote equality of opportunity between men and women. The new integrated duty will also require public authorities to have due regard to the need to foster good relations between men and women.

13.20   As with the race duty, the "unpacking" on the face of the legislation of what is meant by "advancing equality of opportunity" should encourage public authorities to take a more proactive approach.

Impact on gender reassignment

13.21   The current gender equality duty requires public
         authorities to eliminate unlawful discrimination and
         harassment on grounds of gender reassignment). . The
         new integrated duty will also require public authorities to
         have due regard to the need to foster good relations
         between men and women. The new Equality Duty will also
         require public authorities to have due regard to advance
         equality of opportunity and foster good relations between
         people who share the protected characteristic of gender
         reassignment and those who do not.

13.21   The extension of the Duty to gender reassignment should
         encourage public authorities to take a more proactive and
         sensitive approach in dealing with the transsexual
         community.

Impact on disability

13.22   The existing disability equality duty requires public
         authorities to have due regard to the need to:

- eliminate unlawful discrimination;

- eliminate harassment that is linked to a disabled
  person's disabilities;

- promote positive attitudes towards disabled people,
  and

- encourage participation in public life.

13.23 It also requires public authorities to take steps to take account of disabled persons' disabilities, even where that involves treating disabled people more favourably than non-disabled people.

13.24 Each limb of the current disability equality duty is carried over to the new as follows:

Elimination of unlawful discrimination

- The first element of the disability duty requires public authorities to eliminate unlawful discrimination. This is replicated in the first limb of the new Equality Duty.

Elimination of harassment

- The second element of the disability duty requires public authorities to eliminate harassment of disabled people that is linked to a disabled person's disability. Unlawful harassment is caught by the first limb of the new Equality Duty. We still want and intend to catch low-level harassment of disabled people that is short of unlawful harassment, such as name-calling in streets, spitting, ostracism, local residents organising petitions against disabled people moving in to the area and so on.

- The third limb of the Equality Duty will require public authorities to foster good relations, and in particular tackle prejudice and promote understanding. The type of action a public authority might take to counter such low-level yet lawful harassment would be action that falls within this limb of the Equality Duty – such as education campaigns, community meetings and so on. (The same applies to low-level yet lawful harassment of other protected groups – such as gay and lesbian people).

- An explicit reference to tackling prejudice will be easier for public authorities to understand and act on than a reference to tackling lawful harassment. The new formulation should therefore lead to more concrete action to benefit disabled people.

Promotion of equality of opportunity

- The third element of the disability duty requires public authorities to promote equality of opportunity between disabled people and other people. This is covered by the second limb of the new Equality Duty, namely "advance equality of opportunity".

Taking steps to take account of disability, even where that requires treating disabled people more favourably

- The fourth element of the disability duty requires public authorities to have due regard to the need to take steps to take account of disabled persons' disabilities, even where that means treating disabled people more favourably.

- Disability stakeholders indicated that this clarificatory element has been vital in showing public authorities that they can, indeed in some cases must, treat disabled people more favourably. The Government agrees. It is central to the main aim of the expanded duty that public authorities should not treat everybody the same, but should consider treating people differently in order to achieve full equality in practice. The Bill therefore makes clear that compliance with the duty may involve treating some people more favourably than others, within the confines of anti-discrimination law including the particular nature of disability discrimination law. Clear guidance from the Equality and Human Rights Commission will also help to clarify the action public authorities can and should take in this respect.

Promotion of positive attitudes

- The fifth element of the disability duty requires public authorities to consider how to promote positive attitudes towards disabled people. The new requirement for public authorities to consider how to tackle prejudice subsumes and in fact strengthens this protection for disabled people.

Encouraging participation in public life

- The sixth element of the disability duty requires public authorities to encourage participation in public life. In the new Equality Duty, the requirement to have due regard to the need to advance equality of opportunity includes, amongst other things, encouraging participation in all activities where people are under represented, including in public life. This should have a positive impact on disabled people by widening the potential scope of this limb of the new Duty.

Chapter 14:

Positive action

14.1   The Equality Bill will give employers and service providers greater scope to take positive action measures within the boundaries of what is permitted by EU law. It will still retain what is permissible under the current legislation, for instance the provisions that relate to training and encouragement for specific types of work and to particular needs. The new positive action provisions will need to be supported by guidance and possibly a code of practice produced by the Equality and Human Rights Commission.

14.2   It is not clear to what extent the existing positive action measures have been taken up by employers or service providers, as there are no detailed figures. There is some evidence that a number of employers in both the private and public sector have made use of the provisions. But there is also evidence that the existing provisions may be poorly understood.

14.3   The new provisions will be more expansive and less reliant on simple statistical evidence of under-representation before they can be utilised. The guidance that will be produced by the Commission will need to contain practical examples of the types of positive action that employers will be able to take. Taken together, this should give employers more confidence that any positive action interventions that they choose to undertake will be within the law and be likely to achieve the desired outcome.

Stakeholder engagement

14.4   Over 90% of those who responded to the consultation on the Bill were in favour of extending the positive action provisions beyond their current limits.

14.5   From consultation and discussion with equality stakeholders it is apparent that they regard the existing positive action measures as under-used, particularly within the private sector.

14.6   Equality stakeholders generally agree that clarifying and widening the scope of positive action legislation will help:

- Create a more diverse workforce

- Address under-representation of minority groups

- Give employers the confidence to use positive action measures more frequently and more extensively

- Empower public authorities and other service providers to deliver the range of services needed to meet the needs of all sectors of society.

General impact

14.7   Employers and service providers will have greater freedom to address disadvantage such as under-representation in the workforce of, for example, women or black and Asian people. In particular, it will allow employers to take under-representation into account when selecting between two equally suitable candidates.

14.8   The Bill will also permit service providers to target their services to meet the needs of particular groups, such as such as additional healthcare screening for women or information technology training for "silver surfers".

14.9   The use of positive action will be entirely voluntary. However, it can play an important role in helping large organisations to achieve more representative workforces, such as police services which want to increase the number of officers from ethnic minority backgrounds in order to better reflect the communities they serve.

14.10   By enabling employers to establish a more diverse and representative workforce these measures may in turn help organisations to understand more fully the needs of their customers and service users.

14.11   Political parties will also be able use wider positive action measures to tackle under-representation and compensate for disadvantage. For example, individuals from under-represented groups in each of the equality strands may benefit from:

- Targeted mentoring and shadowing schemes;

- Targeted training and leadership programmes;

- Specific committees or sections based on a protected

characteristic (e.g. black sections/forums);

- Specific seats reserved on committees for those from a specific protected ground (for instance women or disabled people).

Impact on gender

14.12   In Parliament there is still a significant under-representation of women (19% of MPs are women compared to 51% of the population).

14.13   It is important to ensure that Parliament, and our other democratic institutions, properly reflect the make-up of our society. The Equality Bill extends to 2030 the period during which women-only electoral shortlists can be used by political parties. Over 90% of consultation responses on this subject agreed to an extension and, in a separate consultation in exercise, it was overwhelmingly agreed that 2030 was the most practical new expiry date. Women-only shortlists have already had a positive impact in increasing the number of women MPs. If current progress is maintained, the extension of the expiry date could lead to approximately 200 women MPs by then.

Chapter 15:

Conclusions

15.1   The Government believes that the provisions in the
        Equality Bill will have a positive impact on all the equality
        strands. The effect will differ according to each strand,
        partly because the rights and protections currently
        available also differ according to each strand. The overall
        impact will be to achieve greater consistency, where
        appropriate. Where provisions are not harmonised, this is
        based on a reasoned proposition.

15.2   There will generally be no regression of existing protection
        overall. The biggest benefit will be for those strands that
        are afforded less protection under current law and for
        whom protection will be extended by the Equality Bill.

Chapter 16:

Monitoring arrangements

16.1   The Equality and Human Rights Commission has a duty,
         under section 11 of the Equality Act 2006, to monitor the
         effectiveness of the equality and human rights
         enactments. It may advise central or devolved
         government about the effectiveness of any of those
         enactments and make recommendations for amendment.

16.2   More broadly, the Equality and Human Rights
         Commission also has a duty to monitor progress towards
         the development of a society in which (under section 3 of
         the Equality Act 2006):

- people's ability to achieve their potential is not limited
  by prejudice or discrimination;

- there is respect for and protection of each individual's
  human rights;

- there is respect for the dignity and worth of each
  individual;

- each individual has an equal opportunity to participate
  in society, and

- there is mutual respect between groups based on
  understanding and valuing of diversity and on shared

respect for equality and human rights.

15.3   The Government will be looking to the Equality and
        Human Rights Commission to monitor the effectiveness of
        the new Equality Act (with the exception of the duty
        regarding socio-economic inequalities).

15.4   Additionally, the Government will conduct a post
        legislative review of the Bill, around five years after Royal
        Assent, which will assess the implementation of the
        legislation and also how the Act has worked in practice, in
        light of its objectives.

15.5   Although post legislative scrutiny in general is not
        designed specifically to focus on equality outcomes and
        monitoring, the very nature and purpose of the Equality
        Bill mean that this will be at the core of the post legislative
        scrutiny process.

Equality Impact Assessment – Association and Perception

The new policy

In the context of the European Court of Justice Coleman judgment in Coleman v. Atrridge Law which was handed down on 17 July 2008 and in accordance with the aim of the Equality Bill to harmonise, where practicable, anti-discrimination legislation, the Government proposes in the Bill to extend protection against direct discrimination and harassment based on association and perception to other equality strands where no or only partial protection currently exists, so that there is a uniform approach across the protected characteristics. Currently, protection against discrimination and harassment already exists for people who associate with or are wrongly perceived to posses characteristics of race, sexual orientation and religion or belief, at work and outside the workplace; and also people wrongly perceived to be a certain age, at work. Protection against harassment with respect to religion and belief or sexual orientation is limited to within the workplace.

Consequently, the Equality Bill will also provide protection against:

i. direct discrimination or harassment in employment and vocational training which arises because of a person's association with a disabled person, or because he/she is falsely perceived to be disabled;

ii. direct discrimination or harassment in the provision of goods, facilities, services, education, premises, clubs, and the functions of public bodies, which arises because of a person's association with a disabled person, or because he/she is falsely perceived to be disabled.

iii. direct discrimination or harassment in the provision of goods, facilities, services, education, premises, clubs, and the functions of public bodies, which arises because of a person's association with a person of a certain age, or because he/she is falsely perceived to be of a certain age, where this is 18 or over.

iv.   direct discrimination or harassment in employment or vocational training which arises because of a person's association with a person of a certain age

v.   direct discrimination in the provision of goods, facilities, services, education, premises, clubs, and the functions of public bodies, which arises because of a person's association with or being falsely perceived as a person of a certain sex or a transsexual person[35].

vi.   direct discrimination in employment or vocational training which arises because of a person's association with or being falsely perceived as a person of a certain sex or a transsexual person.

Equality impact of the policy

There are no data to indicate precisely how many people are associates of disabled people, people of a certain age, sex or of transsexual people. Nor are there any reliable data as to the number of people who might be falsely perceived to possess one of these characteristics. However, in terms of association, these changes will apply to a significant proportion of the population, albeit that most will likely not be required to enforce their new rights. For disability for example, it is estimated that around 13.9 million people will be newly protected on grounds of association and perception. The main impact is likely to be on people who look after or care for older, younger or disabled people.

Positive impact of the policy

In extending discrimination legislation to cover association and perception for all the main protected characteristics, it is considered that the overall impact of the proposed policy should be positive. People who care for others will be protected. The strengthened law will offer greater means of redress for people who suffer less favourable or degrading treatment simply because

---

[35] The term 'transsexual' is used here to describe someone who intends to undergo, is undergoing or has undergone gender reassignment.

they are falsely perceived to be or associate with someone who is of a particular age or disabled or transsexual or a woman.

Extending protection from direct discrimination and harassment based on an association or perception will achieve greater harmonisation across the Bill because this protection already exists in respect of race, sexual orientation, religion or belief, and partially in respect of age (perception in employment). Harmonisation with other equality strands should make the law easier to interpret by courts and tribunals and easier to understand for those with duties under discrimination legislation.

Monitoring

The relative impacts will be assessed through monitoring the volume of tribunal and court cases. Such monitoring will be carried out by the Government Equalities Office, in conjunction with the Equality and Human Rights Commission, as part of the overall monitoring of the impact of the Equality Bill, once enacted.